HOW TO FIND SEA MONSTERS

T0009816

Thomas Kingsley Troupe

BLACK
RABBIT
BOOKS

Hi Jinx is published by Black Rabbit Books
P.O. Box 227, Mankato, Minnesota, 56002.
www.blackrabbitbooks.com
Copyright © 2023 Black Rabbit Books

Marysa Storm, editor; Michael Sellner, designer
and photo researcher

Library of Congress Cataloging-in-Publication Data
Names: Troupe, Thomas Kingsley, author.
Title: How to find sea monsters / by Thomas Kingsley Troupe.
Description: Mankato : Black Rabbit Books, [2023] |
Series: Hi jinx. paranormal field guides | Includes bibliographical references
and index. | Audience: Ages 8-12 | Audience: Grades 4-6 |
Summary: "With fun facts, a colorful design, and critical thinking questions,
How to Find Sea Monsters inspires readers to take their love of the paranormal
to the next level all while laughing and learning"– Provided by publisher.
Identifiers: LCCN 2020034527 (print) | LCCN 2020034528 (ebook) |
ISBN 9781623107192 (hardcover) | ISBN 9781644665688 (paperback) |
ISBN 9781623107253 (ebook)
Subjects: LCSH: Sea monsters–Juvenile literature.
Classification: LCC GR910 .T76 2022 (print) | LCC GR910 (ebook) |
DDC 001.944–dc23
LC record available at https://lccn.loc.gov/2020034527
LC ebook record available at https://lccn.loc.gov/2020034528

Image Credits

Dreamstime: Sven Bachstroem, 8–9; iStock: 1ndependent,
Cover, 19; davidnay, Cover, 19; Shutterstock: Aleksandr
Bryliaev, 14; Anton Balazh, 14; Arcady, 12; bogadeva1983,
2–3; Christos Georghiou, Cover, 19; ekler, 16; Framework
Wonderland, Cover, 1, 18–19, 21; Galyna G, 3, 4, 7, 12, 17,
18, 19; HitToon, Cover, 1; jdrv_art, 12–13; LOMAKIN, 23;
Lorelyn Medina, 7, 18; March13, 1, 21; mejnak, 5; Memo
Angeles, 5, 12, 13; monbibi, 5, 6, 14; Morphart Creation,
10; My Life Graphic, 5, 10, 18–19; Nikolayev Alexey, 20;
NoPainNoGain, 7; Oliver Denker, 17; OShaptala, 14, 21;
Pasko Maksim, 23, 24; Pitju, 4, 8, 11, 17, 21; Ron Dale, 3, 4,
8, 15, 20; totallypic, 5, 7; zooco, 5

CONTENTS

Chapter 1
ON THE HUNT

If you're reading this book, that can mean only one thing! You want to find sea monsters. Many have tried. Most have failed. A few have even disappeared. I'm guessing they were eaten by something from the deep. Or maybe they were grabbed by big, slimy **tentacles**.

Not scared yet? Good. You might just have what it takes. I've seen all kinds of sea monsters in my travels. This field guide you're holding will help you find some too!

Thomas Kingsley Troupe

Thomas Kingsley Troupe is not well-known for his sea monster research. But he sure loves talking about the creatures. He claims to have seen thousands of sea monsters. We asked for proof, but he only showed us drawings. He said his camera was lost at sea.

Handy and Helpful

Since you're not a salty sea dog like me, you'll need help hunting sea monsters. That's where my field guide comes in. This book covers everything sea monster. You'll know what they look like and what they eat for breakfast. You'll learn where to find them too!

So pack your bags. And keep this book close. It'll be almost like you and I are on the hunt together. I just won't have to smell your puke if you get seasick! *

*Expert's Note
You might want to bring a barf bag.

midnight zone

The sea is divided into layers of depth. One of the deeper layers is called the midnight zone. If there are sea monsters, they probably live down there.

Chapter 2

CREATURE CHARACTERISTICS

To find sea monsters, you need to know what you're looking for. Luckily for us, there are all kinds of **nautical** nasties to search for. Some look like giant sea snakes with scales and fins. Others, such as the kraken, look like huge octopuses. These monsters are bigger than most boats.

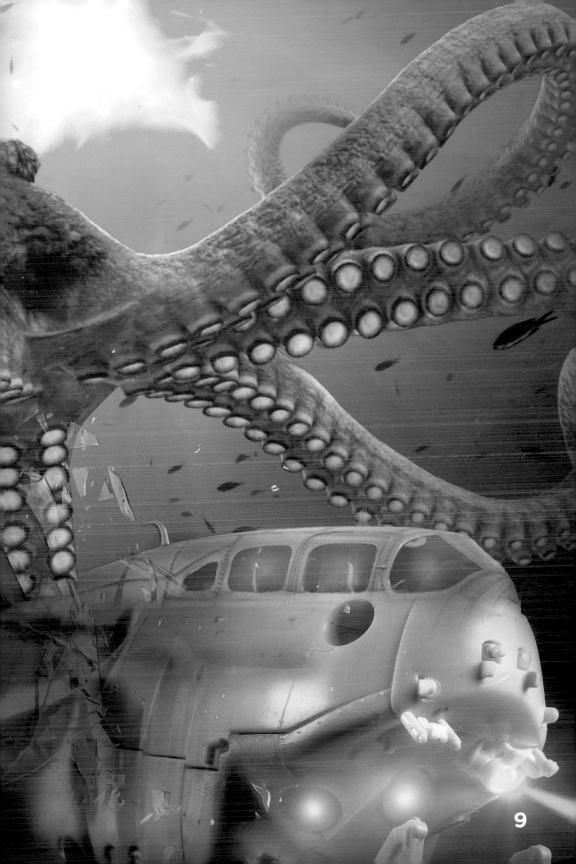

Behaviors

Most people go their whole lives without seeing a sea monster. I think it's because the beasties are shy. They like to be by themselves. But if they feel bothered or **threatened**, watch out! I've seen them pull entire ships underwater. Others breathe fire and heat water until it begins to boil.

Diet

Sea monsters need a lot of food for their giant bodies. Often, they'll inhale anything in their paths. Fish, octopuses, sharks, and people on Jet Skis all become meals.

I think these creatures are tired of seafood, though. Imagine eating cake your entire life. Sounds awful. Something tells me they'd love a simple ham sandwich for a change.*

*Expert's Note

A nice turkey wrap might work well too.

*Expert's **Note**

Check out lakes too. That's right! Not all sea monsters live in the sea.

BERMUDA TRIANGLE

Some animals that live in dark water create their own light. If there are sea monsters, they might do this too.

14

Chapter 3

WHERE TO FIND THEM

Most experts will tell you the same thing. If you want to find sea monsters, you need to search the sea.* But the seas are HUGE. Where do you even begin? Try the places ships have disappeared. If you're really feeling **gutsy**, explore the **Bermuda Triangle**. Some people think monsters cause disappearances there.

Tracking the Creatures

It's not easy tracking a creature that doesn't leave footprints. Your best bet is to watch the water. Study how the water ripples. There could be something beneath the surface. If you're brave, you can dive into the deep. If all else fails, throw a ham sandwich into the water and step back!

A giant squid's body can be longer than a school bus. Now just imagine how big a sea monster could be!

Approaching the Creatures

What should you do when you find a sea monster? **Avoid** eye contact. Steer clear of any tentacles too. Then start up a friendly conversation. Tell them you like how they smell. Maybe ask what boats taste like. Just act natural!

Before you say it, yes, you're welcome for all my help. Thanks to me, you now know how to find sea monsters!

Chapter 4

GET IN ON THE HI JINX

Sea monsters from stories might not be real. But people discover new sea creatures all the time. You can see some of these for yourself! Visit zoos and aquariums. Explore the library to find books about sea creatures. Read articles on the Internet. Maybe someday, you'll discover new sea creatures. Who knows? One might even be a sea monster.

Take It One Step More

1. Stories describe many types of sea monsters. What kind would scare you the most? Describe it.

2. Why do you think people started telling stories about sea monsters? Research to find out.

3. Pretend you've captured a sea monster. Would you release it or sell it to a zoo?

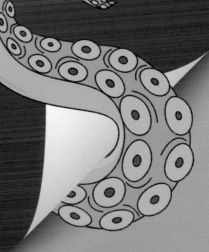

GLOSSARY

avoid (uh-VOYD)—to keep away from

Bermuda Triangle (ber-MYOO-duh TRAHY-ang-guhl)—a triangular area in the North Atlantic Ocean that is the site of numerous reported disappearances of planes and ships

claim (KLAYM)—to say something is true when some people might say it's not true

gutsy (GUHT-see)—very tough or brave

nautical (NAW-ti-kuhl)—relating to ships and sailing

tentacle (TEN-tuh-kuhl)—a long, flexible arm

threatened (THRET-uhnd)—having an uncertain chance of continued survival

LEARN MORE

BOOKS

Braun, Eric. *Taking Care of Your Sea Monster.* Caring for Your Magical Pets. Mankato, MN: Black Rabbit Books, 2020.

Ransom, Candice. *Mysterious Loch Ness Monster.* Spooked! Minneapolis: Lerner Publications, 2021.

Troupe, Thomas Kingsley. *Sea Serpents.* Mythical Creatures. Minneapolis: Bellwether Media, 2021.

WEBSITES

8 Fun Facts about Deep-Sea Monsters
www.scholastic.com/teachers/lesson-plans/ teaching-content/8-fun-facts-about-deep-sea- monsters/

Ocean Habitat Facts and Photos
kids.nationalgeographic.com/explore/nature/ habitats/ocean/

Sea Serpent-Kids
kids.britannica.com/kids/article/sea-serpent/ 390052

INDEX